[INSERT] BOY

Danez Smith

[INSERT] BOY

YESYES BOOKS PORTLAND

[INSERT] BOY © 2014 BY DANEZ SMITH

COVER ART: "MAN WITH CAT" © 2014 JONATHAN CHASE
INTERIOR ART: "THE SILENCE'S LOVER" © 2014 JONATHAN CHASE
COVER AND BOOK DESIGN BY ALBAN FISCHER

FIRST EDITION, 2014
SECOND PRINTING, 2015
ISBN 978-1-936919-28-4
PRINTED IN THE UNITED STATES OF AMERICA

PUBLISHED BY YESYES BOOKS
4904 NE 29TH AVE
PORTLAND, OR 97211
YESYESBOOKS.COM

KMA SULLIVAN, PUBLISHER
HEATHER BROWN, PUBLICIST
MARY CATHERINE CURLEY, DIRECTOR OF SOCIAL MEDIA
MARK DERKS, FICTION EDITOR, *VINYL*
STEVIE EDWARDS, ACQUISITIONS EDITOR
ALBAN FISCHER, GRAPHIC DESIGNER
JILL KOLONGOWSKI, MANAGING EDITOR
JOHN MORTARA, WEB DESIGN AND MANAGEMENT
PHILLIP B. WILLIAMS, POETRY EDITOR, *VINYL*
JOANN BALINGIT, ASSISTANT EDITOR
BEYZA OZER, ASSISTANT EDITOR
AMBER RAMBHAROSE, ASSISTANT EDITOR
CARLY SCHWEPPE, INTERN, *VINYL*
ROBERT WHITEHEAD, ASSISTANT EDITOR, *VINYL*

for the Smiths & the Pattersons
who held me up & kept me going

"…*It was so outrageous you couldn't go any further*
& so you had to find a way to use it."

—JAMES BALDWIN ON BEING POOR, BLACK, AND GAY

BLACK BOY BE

like ocean hid behind a grain of sand

like a village ablaze & dreaming of spit

like ashy hands bathed in blue flame

like a pillar of bones sealed by honey

like a mouthless prayer, a lost glory

like a gold watch slowed by blood

like blood all over everything: the reeboks,
the tube socks, the air & the mother's hands

like a nothing at all, & ain't that something?

ain't that the world?

THE BLACK BOY & THE BULLET

one is hard & the other tries to be

    one is fast & the other is faster

        one is loud & one is a song
        with one note & endless rest

        one's whole life is a flash

    both spend their life trying to find someone
    to hold them bloodwarm & near

both spark the same debate
some folks want to protect them/some think we should just get rid
                of the damn things all together.

ALTERNATE NAMES FOR BLACK BOYS

1. smoke above the burning bush
2. nemesis of summer night
3. first son of soil
4. coal awaiting spark & wind
5. guilty until proven dead
6. oil heavy starlight
7. monster until proven ghost
8. gone
9. boy
10. phoenix who forgets to un-ash
11. god of shovels & black veils
12. what once passed for kindling
13. fireworks at dawn
14. brilliant, shadow colored coral
15. (I thought to leave this blank
    but who am I to name us nothing?)
16. prayer who learned to bite & sprint
17. a mother's joy & clutched breath

FOR BLACK BOYS

you wade through your people's gun smoke

from a battle nobody ever named

more than *struggle*.

white folks are afraid when you speak.

hot wound where your mouth should be

where you see God: they see tin man
made from prison bars
gorilla trained to shoot.

you are a heavenless thing to them,

wings made of pork bone

a halo grown tired & fat

tight around your neck.

How do you describe a son set
course to casket from birth?

The grim reaper is named Ray-Ray.
He's your cousin, has tears
inked into his cheek
because no one told him
he was beautiful enough
to cry. He has a talent
for making ghost.

came out the womb obituary scribed on the backside of your birth certificate. you're nothing new. they've seen this before. you're a rerun, a dull flash in this earth. lightning in a ghost town. Mama told you to hit anybody who hits you first. you walked outside throwing fist at air. this is how you fight the world back. vaseline making a diamond of your skin & nobody saying you're pretty. grow up, throw knuckle & metal into boys down the block or round the corner. race to make each other more ugly, less diamond, more dead. a cold black boy body is a prophecy fulfilled. you have always been a dying thing.

Sean Bell got filled with a war's worth of lead
& the marriage rates went up

    Bo Morrison got killed with his hands up
    & people invested in garages

Oscar Grant was slain, belly pressed to the floor
& I need a Tide-To-Go pen for this stain

    Trayvon Martin got his light drained
    & everybody tasted the rainbow

Latasha Harlins died over OJ
& I still need a pack of cigarettes from the store

    10 Black girls went missing & you found your keys
    10 Black boys died & mama said *kids these days*

10 Black boys got shot outside the schoolhouse
& everybody got one extra fry at lunch

I am sorry I have no happy poems
about the ashy hallelujah of knees.
Whenever I open my mouth, ghosts raid

my poor tongue demanding names. I say
Devonte & my mouth drips stray braids.
I say *Keshawn* & vomit gold teeth.

It's always like this, my one good song
still unclaimed at the morgue, my hands
try to clap & end up cupping a skull.

FAGGOT
OR WHEN THE FRONT GOES UP

feathers for muscles. jawline of pearls.
fire set mauve & spinning.
beast of berry-stained claw. teeth littered
with petal & cotton. hymn for skin.

a boy made of sunflowers.
more tomboy than boy.
preferred the dress to the plastic gun.
pined for pink to grace your soft black back.

you were never your grandfather's boy.
his first words were fist.
he cackled at bruise & burn.
you were a sweeter thing. a delicate sun.

then he called you that word enough
& you turned action figure. tumble
& punch brained. blood on the knees
& under nails

not yours. a boy made of war.
a boy who swung to keep from singing.

GENESISSY

for Dwayne "Gully Queen" Jones & Islan Nettles

& on the eighth day, god said *let there be fierce* & that's the story about the first snap, the hand's humble attempt at thunder, a small sky troubled by attitude // & on the ninth day, God said *Bitch, werk* & Adam learned to duck walk, dip, pose, death drop, Eve became the fruit herself, stared lions in the eye & dared to bite // & on the tenth day, God wore a blood red sequin body suit, dropped it low, named it Sunset // & on the eleventh day God said *guuuurrrrrl* & trees leaned in for gossip, water went wild for the tea, & the airtight with shade // & on the twelfth day, Jesus wept at the mirror, mourning the day his sons would shame his sons for walking a daughter's stride, for the way his children would learn to hate the kids // & on the thirteenth day, God barely moved, he laid around dreaming of glitter; pleased with the shine, sad so many of his children would come home covered in it, parades canceled due to rain of fist & insults & rope & bullets // & on the fourteenth day God just didn't know what to do with himself the lord begat man man begat sin   sin begat a new joy

a new joy begat hate hate begat Leviticus Leviticus begat Sista Rose

Sista Rose begat that ugly rumor

     ugly rumor begat the truth

         truth begat the need to pray or run

the need to run begat the knees
(& that is a kind of praying too)

     the knees begat the mouth splattered
     across him-colored dirt road

         the mouth splattered across her
         -colored dirt road still begat song

song begat hymns at the sweet "boy's" funeral

     the sweet girl's funeral begat
     her aunt's disgusted head shake

his aunt's disgusted head shake
begat the world that killed
the not a boy-child
& stole her favorite dress
right off her cold shimmering body
& that can't come from God right?

& MY MOTHER NOTICES SOMEONE
ELSE'S BLOOD ON MY HANDS

is that paint? she asked of the slender
swirls making my knuckles pretty.
I said no hoping she wouldn't dig

into my hands' war-stained glamor.
Sunshine all over my fist (no I did
not uppercut the sky, pull back a mess

of hot bright bones). I struck a light
skinned boy with chamomile eyes
who tried to steal my wallet

out my FUBU jeans folded on the side
of our crumbling court. blood stains my ring
finger, marries me to each cut on his face

& the purple pregnant swell of his body.
What did you eat? & I wanted to tell her
I ate a boy's pride covered in ranch & hot sauce

I gobbled my own laugh, deep for the first time
while he fell to the ground, I ran, greedy
for my own sweet life when Sunshine went to tell

his brothers, our neighborhood Goliaths,
who pined for pain, not names. I knew my name
was not David. I didn't speak a word

to my mom, just walked past her, praying
she said nothing as I'm sure a man had done
to her before. I didn't go to the court for two weeks.

When I did, no one spoke of my victory
or cowardice, we just hooped. That's all
we wanted to be there for.

A FAILED ATTEMPT AT CREATION

I walked around
stuffing my pockets
with snow from the grooves
of tires, the middle
of the street & bottom steps.
I built a man in my image,
gave him a hat, a good pair
of loafers, a dime bag, everything
I've learned about being black,
holy, drunk, my mother's son,
not afraid of the gun
& he looked more
like stone when I was done.
I was so sure he'd see August,
but like his maker
he could only fight so long.
I'm happy I didn't
give him a face. I couldn't
look into his eyes. I couldn't
hear him scream.

[PAPA'S LIL']

ALL SPRING, WE'D WATCH GRANDPA RUB HIS KNEE & COMPLAIN ABOUT RAIN

& then it was summer & our porch would be full of men
with names like June Bug, Turnip Seed, & Delroy

who were uncles either by blood or blood-shed, who demanded
water, corn liquor, & catfish, who we mixed brandy-cokes for

in the kitchen, who let us savor the sweet burn
& joggled us on their knees, who filled themselves

with moonshine & sloe gin & smoke & never seemed to put down
their dominoes, who beat their wives because their fathers did,

who never touched their wives after their sons grew shoulders
wide enough to break a spine, who loved their wives

enough to never call them the other's name, who never stepped
foot in church, who asked their sisters to pray for them, who wept

when their daughters hummed gospel, who worked three jobs
to barely afford rice, who fled their homes Saturday nights

filled with too much of the devil's brown blood & names
of brothers left to twirl from the limbs of those poplars,

who we feared as much as we loved, whose backs we washed
when they couldn't, whose lips we brought water to

when their hands became fresh dust, who we begged to sprint
towards the light & dance there, who we swore to never speak ill of

& promised we'd never be.

"AN OLD MAN COUGHS AND HACKS UP A DEAD BODY, I THINK IT'S HIS FORMER SELF"

—THOMAS HILL

I don't know, Thomas. I too have seen this scene. My grandfather coughs all night as the wrecked limbs of ghost bloom from his throat. They climb out from the war that still deploys his dreams. They stare at him, some of them soldiers with half their skulls blown into pink dust, some of them charred mothers holding the air where a child's hand used to be. They stare at him & they do not counterattack or haunt, they sing, they cry, they spend all night with my grandfather telling each other the tales of their first loves & telling each other *I Love You*. Thomas, I have seen a man love what is dead because of his hands. I have seen white men in Mississippi weeping near tall trees. I have seen couples sit by the playground with no child of their own. Thomas, my grandfather's mouth is crowded with the dead. He knows not their names, but sings their prayers in perfect Vietnamese. He chants until the soft red dawn, until his tongue is bloody with their old music, trying to save his soul from what was required of his hands.

SWAYLESS

I guess I've never seen my grandma dance
But I've seen her cook, seen her dodge

I wonder if my grandfather's hands
Were a dance floor instead of an armory

Would she pause, if it caught in the ghost
Or a choke, & unleash those handed down hips

I wonder what song would have to play
To make her a black blur of joy & pepper mane

I wonder if she has any music at all

MY GRANDMA USED TO TELL MY GRANDFATHER *JUST GO TO HELL*

& I'm so scared he listened

TO MY GRANDFATHER'S PROSTATE CANCER

you awoke dressed as a rose blooming
with blades, an untamed garden of tulips & fly traps
sprawled your name across his most untouched
commanded his body to bow & smell your sweet

acid, your slow & reckless violence
you bully of the bully, turned a monster
into a man into a boy into a puddle
of want begging to be held

how did you do it? replaced my grandmother's face
with your swell of carnivorous pink matter
replaced the man we knew with the man we knew could be
I will not curse you for proving him delicate

I will not damn you for whisking him away to dance
with dirt. for what you took, you gave us six years of soft
tinged joy, hands who could touch without bruising
oh sweet sick, I want to kiss you all over

your red velvet mouth, speak all your names back into you:

> *hot pink undertaker, Hades of the underskin*
> *tiny knot of mercy, God of growth & rapid weight loss*
> *impossible hero, Lord of a decaying kingdom*
> *the first time I saw my grandfather hold his wife's hand*
> *first time his open palm did not demand blood*

SHIT

a puddle under what's left
of you. you are half my size,

a quarter your own.
can't control your bowels, your hands,

your eyes. through a mirror
I see you leak. I know you'd rather

me watch you make waste than shed tears.
pride is a wicked mistress

for a man made of kindling
&, often, too many fist. it's come to this:

a night gown, hospice, the door wide open
for what you used to click the lock for.

now, my hand on what remains
of your back, the other in what you wouldn't

even let a woman touch.
I can't say a word.

who could even think of saying? maybe
if I knew you less, or if I wasn't so sure

this silence was prayed for, I'd whisper, *go ahead.*
let your body do its work. let me do mine.

[RUINED]

THE ROAD KILL & MY BODY

The difference is the deer, somewhere
between severed & smashed, did not limp
back to his quiet home

    The difference is the boy was not a car

The difference is I saw it coming slowly

        The difference is I was told thank you after

The difference is half of a deer
blood emptied & insides
fashioned into a skirt
is still called a deer

    A man, emptied of his voice
    & drawers echoing a red terrible song
    is called a myth or a bitch or not a man at all.

HEALING: ATTEMPT #1

it escape me like a plague of snakes   *choke me*   & my neck is a beggar
& his hands are a holiday & I hope the spirit hits him. I pray to be gifted no air,
for his hands to ribbon my throat, for the knot to pull tighter & tighter until his
palms touch & he wonders if I was even there. I get my wish, & my eyes flutter to
white, & my lungs are two bears skinned & decorating the fireplace, & my lungs
are boxes full of wet dust, & my lungs are empty as a cathedral on a Tuesday night,
& outside the window Panama is a girl dancing covered in church bells. the bells fill
the room, my spirit leaves me, the room goes black & I wake up soaked in myself
& he is crying too.

HEALING: ATTEMPT #2

I pray to each god I know: the one who sends his son to the people who greet him with stones, the one who dresses as a swan & uses storms to burn skirts off, the one who promises that I will come back as an eagle or a roach. yeah, maybe I should give my throat over to prayer or offer it up as a sacrifice or something, maybe they all want me to say ahhhhh or amen. who knows. most gods are just another man who demands my knees & I know where that commandment leads.

UNTITLED AND ABOUT SADNESS

define *danger*.   a black boy
quiet in his bed with his thoughts after
recurring dreams of the medicine cabinet.

define *fear*.   that same boy
in that same bed hours later in the same
position afraid of dreaming the same dream.

define *worry*.   his mother
his friends. his God. the woman on the bus
who mourned at the sight of him.

HEALING: ATTEMPT #3

one time I begged a man to hold me fully clothed while I mended my broken song back into the hymn I owned before him & his hands & whatever else I am supposed to say to make you know that my body was once not mine & barely is today. If I told you his name, I'm afraid you might offer him water. If I drew his face, I worry you might frame it in your bedroom. He was a beautiful boy, the one who stole me. He was my type: strong, black, alive. He smelled so holy, like a sacrifice burning nearby.

MAYBE THEY'RE NOT HOLY,
MAYBE THEY'RE JUST YOUR HANDS

I say your name & a church lurches
from my throat, one 4x4 at a time

dragging its nails along my pink.
I like the pain. I beg for it, the whole while

pews spilling between my teeth. my teeth.
I can't picture your hands unscarlet now.

a brick wall color of my brick colored skin
spotted with the knuckles' thin wine.

you ain't touched me same since I found out
you too are a war-maker, my soft sanctuary reborn

a gun range, your foreplay cramped
with brass shells. why, my God?

the book says my first God made you
in his image & I've read the whole thing.

let me tell you the wrath you're capable of

HEALING: ATTEMPT #4

I drive around the city, killing everyone who looks like him in my head: the boys with skin the color of burnt wire, the men with shoulders threatening to become wings, the people who smile, the ones who steal candy & eat it right in the store. no one is safe in my dream drive-by. Tarantino would love this shit, it's the perfect revenge flick: the boy who kills everyone just for fitting the description of his blood-song, who shoots his path to peace all the way from Minnesota to Panama, who considers the gun his flesh & his law, who avoids mirrors, large bodies of water, & looking at his own hands for if he saw his reflection he'd have to off that nigga too.

HEALING: ATTEMPT #5

I know he's black by the way he calls me a bitch. I know he is tall for I've spurned my neck in a fit of hunger & worship. & what is worship without a song stopped up in the throat & choking the choir boy blue? & what is worship without an unseen God to bow to? & what kind of servant would I be without prayer? so because I must praise, praise the blindfold for keeping my new Lord from being ruined by sight. praise his easy commandments: *open, spit, & don't use your fucking hands.* praise the darkness of myself where I sit, patient to be the offering & the collection plate. praise his beautiful face I've never seen, for if this one hurt me at least I wouldn't know how much we look like brothers.

[RENT]

THE BUSINESS OF SHADOWS

once, I was almost not there
enough for him to think he was

doing it himself. my mouth: a cave
a wet shelter, a soft temple
to sacrifice what he was glad to rid.

he forgot to say thank you,
but gave me his quick sap & my coins
while cradled in the midst of teeth.

don't ask me to recall his name.
I've always been all tongue, barely a brain.

I keep lists, but nothing like: *James, Donovan, Michael.*
more like: *salt, unripe limes, nickel, mustard, nothing.*

10 RENTBOY COMMANDMENTS
OR THEN THE WHITE GUY
CALLS YOU A NIGGER

but not just any white guy, the one
who's paying you, & not just any nigger,
but his little nigger child. (*never let*
a fifty dollar trick do hundred dollar shit.)
you can't deny he owns you for at least
as long as you are still deep & black
in him. (*remember the terms discussed.*)
so what do you know now? (*if you failed*
to discuss, know anything goes.) you know
he thinks of you as a lion or AIDS
or anything scary & African. (*when anything*
goes, don't panic.) you know he thinks of you
as his son, which makes you scared
for his son, the thought that he could
want anything sweet to be this wild
& trenched in him. (*dazzle him, even while*
soft inside him.) he still called you a nigger,
but so what? You still gonna get paid.
(*respect or groceries?*) you still gonna answer
next time he call. (*this is money.*) you still
broke? Still piss (on him) poor? you got clothes

on your back, brandy in your coffee mug.
(*drink.*) is it worth it to stop this history
if you ain't you gonna eat?
(*pray soon.*) but this is all after thought,
it takes you ten seconds longer than him
to realize your hands around his throat, ten
more for you to notice white mess
on his stomach, ten more for you to cum too.
(*customers must always leave satisfied.*)

MAIL

Dear Mrs. Thompson,

Sorry if you ever taste salt when you kiss your husband
good morning. I hope I didn't taint your coffee or make
a murder of your lipstick. I killed your marriage
& you deserve to know he is not everything you prayed for
but maybe his kiss morning is enough.

Dear Thompson,

Your ATM code is 9976. Your family owns one Honda,
one Ford, all three of your children have bikes. You have
a fireplace, three copies of People Magazine, at the top of
the stairs your children's room is to the left, guest bed to
the right, your room straight ahead, all your walls are white,
everything smells of lavender, you have really nice sheets.

Dear Mrs. Thompson,

Your husband pays me fifty extra dollars when I bust
on his face, twenty five more when I kiss him after. I've never
seen a man grin so hard. He never brushes his teeth. Can you
taste his dinner? Did I bitter the back of your tongue?

Dear Mrs. The Bitch (as he calls you),

I imagine your scalp adorned with three hundred grey follicles,
one for every dead president your man slaps against my chest,
his cash: a tithe, his ass: a cheap offering. I'm sorry for being
so holy to him.

To Whom This May Concern,

Have you ever wondered why it takes him so long to get dressed?
His outfit must be perfect, able to disguise. He can't leave the
closet until he can't recognize himself.

Dear Woman,

You look lovely in the pictures next to the bed he turns face down.

Dear, Dear, Dear Sweet Woman,

I feel we are family now. Caution the way
his waist whines & lips part in his sleep.

Dear Mrs. Thompson,

I fuck your husband twice a week.
He pays me.
He is lying   next to you.

Dear You,

He called me your name once, Ann.

CRAIGSLIST HOOK-UPS

n. 61

forgive me father for I have called another man daddy.
forgive me father for I have worshiped at his denim altar.

forgive me father for I have begged him to bless me
with what he saw fit to bless me with (I showered after).
forgive me father for I have knelt

beside my bed with an open mouth. forgive me
if it looked like prayer, for giving away your mouth.
here lord, take my tongue.

take the black of my gums. take eight teeth.
take my top lip. take the space between my tonsils.
I stuffed them in my throat

to make it easier for you to take them home.
this is my offering. do what you will: build a fire,
feed pigeons, leave them

on the front step of the last man I called your name
while I let him soil your vestibule.

n. 48

cue two bodies veiled in twilight & ember glow,
a body on top of three-fifths a body, a man

& his property enjoying a quiet evening, a man
who can't speak & a man that dare not.

cue Mississippi, dusk & moonshine breath,
a white sheet on the bed, a white sheet on the floor

snatched off by brown hungry hands in need
of being choked, the condoms in the dresser

next to the noose, kisses that taste like wet
red soot, a burnt boy with a heartbeat

like running, his breath stalled by flesh, tongue
a sloppy chorus of *sir yes, please & thank you*,
his mind wild with history & skin, his body confused
whether to attack or cum, for this is not the first time

a white man called him a nigger

in bed, but the first time he asked him
to say it again.

n. 37

When I say your name, you say mine.
When I say *conquer*, you say *resist*.

I'LL SPARE YOU ANOTHER
POEM ABOUT MY MOUTH

instead, here's the story he told me after about the man shot down the street for walking up to the wrong house. well, not really. the man he walked up on, after calling 9 1 1, realized his guest wanted neither cash, jewels, or blood, but help & possibly directions. One panicked officer & kicked down door later, the man was dead. cops came in bullet first.

'& he was white!'   the twist.

he said no more. I asked no more. I won't tell you what he was thinking because I don't know, but maybe he felt like me, skin too taut to bone, small bullet of air in lodged throat, trying not to think what it means for us if they start treating the whites black.

OBEY

at the orgy I deem all the whisky & all the weed & all the coke mine mine mine
& I dare a motherfucker to tell me different. but who would? they line up next to
the free hummus for a shot at the young, black rampage who has come to conquer
the house full of men who could be mall Santas or Senators, except for the brown
one who speaks no English except *yes* & *no* & *harder*. the latter is his favorite, he
makes it my pet name. tonight, I am no one's pet, maybe an animal, wounded &
hungry for revenge or sympathy, but what's the difference? Some white guy says
fuck him, dawg. & I hear *fuck him, dog*. I obey. when the brown one says *no harder*
where I am sure he means stop, I no harder. he kisses his beast on the cheek, walks
away bleeding, smiling, & the blood makes everyone want me more. one by one
they bend, one by one I wreck them. everything must leave here limping & bruised.
everyone must know what I know.

[LOVER]

A LIFE AGO, I WAS A LAKE

was always mouth

open, mouth deep
—blue, a toothless swallow
beautiful, wet cemetery

for the gilled & unblessed
busy with fish & failed limbs.

I still don't know if I died.

they say   *the life you are born*
                  as water is the life
                  you never stop living.

                  (who says that?
                  I have no idea.
                  work with me.)

what was water
has blossomed
to blood, the fish
now anti-body.

my body, once a spot,
now everywhere, hungry
for what hungers for air.

don't let this
fickle flesh fool you.

I can still be all
that damn water.

cut me down
the center. watch
the room flood.

FROM MY WINDOW

you know Lake Mendota still sings
under its frozen flesh in January.

you know you can't wash a song out.
you know the salt boiled out of the dead

sea in summer makes some kind of music
when it swallows the feet of a couple

of kids playing in the sand,
no clue one day they will anchor,
drown, wade swollen blue to shore.

I thought to warn them but who am I to ruin
the best hurt they'll ever know?

what is love without good reason
to fear or run? what is a lake

if its waves do not hum?
what is the skin's saline water

with no one left to savor?
what is a song if no one will sing it

into an ear they've memorized
the taste of?

WARMING

wish I could damn smog & smoke melting the sky away, but it's March & I was
sweating at work. on the way a woman smiled at me walking slow enough to let
wind mull her thighs for the first time since September & I lost myself in the eyes
of a brown boy who looked at me like I was tea his aunt poured over ice & lemon
for him. today should be laced in frost & snow up to our thighs, but instead I am
in bed with a man I barely know & it's too hot to move anymore & I spoke to my
woman & the phone scorched my ear. isn't this beautiful? summer backed winter
into the corner of the calendar. the whole city gave its skin to the god of sun &
damp cotton. somewhere a white bear is floating away on a throne of ice & that
too is gorgeous in its own frightening way.

DANCING (IN BED) WITH
WHITE MEN (WITH DREADS)

Audre, the master's tools brought my house down.
I begged him with my own hands. I've been floorboards,
wing nuts & slow blues at his pale hard feet. his full moon

flesh my new moon flesh, his braided glued yarned
unwashed attack against our tentacled blaze
is pulled sugar to my mouth. Lorde, he doesn't know

how long it takes to look the mirror in the eye,
love what the world won't. Lorde, forgive me
for not grabbing the shears the night

I let him stay in my bed after he said race wasn't real.
Lorde, there are brown boys I never called back
plump, sun descended men, but none of them made me fail

as joyous, none of them so undid my spine's subtle tension.
Lorde, we just didn't relate past our hued past & isn't that
what uppity people say? Is my name's new spelling T-O-M?

I want to tell you about the president. I don't want to tell you
about being four & playing with white barbies,
about frat parties in Wisconsin, the fake black bodies

made discoballs, about rent & the men who paid it for a while,
their wrinkling ghosting bodies, about Chicago & how she bleed,
& still, Lorde, his hair. What is your word? he's in my bed,

dreads splayed, taking up too much space. Audre, gravity is pulling me
everywhere. I sit on the edge. if I fall, I'm not sure where I'll go.

POEM WHERE I BE A DOE & YOU, BY EFFECT, ARE A WOLF

lay me down on eye-white snow

       my slow brooding bed of robin wings

my body slit & smearing everywhere.

       I will not name this new opening a wound.

here, there is no pain I didn't beg for.

       I heard the howl, didn't dare run.

stood waiting for the sweet blades

       of jaw & claw. you found me

wasted no time making a myth

       of my thigh, my flesh turned to wind

the earth under me wet with my life.

I pray this is what they mean by always

that heaven is a persistent mouth.

Baby, I want you forever this way:

fangs covered in me, moon dyed red

bouncing off front teeth, my body

only certain how to twitch, your belly

round with my joy.

CUE THE GANGSTA RAP
WHEN MY KNEES BEND

because my mouth is a whip
& other times my mouth is a whip, you know

bass, rubber, leather seats, detailed flame
you know, some comfy, show-offy shit

fit for music. because he rides me
easy as Sunday, no church

or plate to get to, just cruise, just eight
oh, eight inches of tar

for me to glide & boom. because it's a drug
& always violence & we hood all day

& the only word my mouth cares for is O,
& the only music the kind that kills.

POEM WHERE I BE & YOU JUST MIGHT

I am sitting next to you & you are not there
you're a frameless heat, mass of ruptured air.

to be clear, you are the spit & liver it takes
to be human & I want it & I think you want me

to have it all, but I know
what it's like to be one of the few blacks

for miles. I know what our people think
about me, or maybe us. I know

God's flaming eye, I stare into it always
dying to blink, irises cracking like commandment stones.

I get it.
I get it.

& it might be how you say
my name like a testimony

or how I graze your hand
& yours doesn't move, but my body

made up a rumor about your body
& wants to prove it true. forgive him.

POEM WHERE I BE A HOUSE,
HENCE, YOU LIVE IN ME

hell with your keys! you press paw into my varnished bark

    & all my doors surrender. pace in my rum-soaked carpet

        tumble down my stairs made of gums & the space between

teeth, which means you've stalked my throat

    cast as a spotted beast bulleting towards his feast

        I play a gazelle with a mouth bursting with knives

which means I am a house that swallows

    anything that dares to blood & rise. child, don't play

        in me too long. I've never been a tidy chapel. spotlessness

is for another kind of salvation. I am all mud & mud, I am

    sick of the word *all*, but, baby, everything in me needs

to be wiped down, yet I refuse. leave your print

everywhere, when I'm ready to be clean

I'll burn down.

RAW

I've spent all day trying to come

    up with a metaphor for barebacking.

I've tried face against abrupt winter,

    sockless feet against velvet floors,

punching a warm beast with paper skin;

    none of them work. I don't want to talk

about the risk because I don't want to

    think about risk. miss me with that

chatter about what I know is wrong. I know

    the bones I could become, I know the story

& the other one too, how people disappeared

    mid-sentence in the '80s, how NYC became

a haunted bowl of dust. I know the monster

waiting to pounce my blood, but I wasn't in

my right mind, I was barely in my body at all.

I CAST OUT MY TONGUE LIKE A KEY

aren't we an anomaly?
    body, just uppity wind,

pressure system who doesn't
    know when to leave. I am warm

front knocked up against
    brick wall, his body is fresh

from the Canadian hills
    there's a tornado all up in my mouth

ruining my teeth, leaving
    nothing behind but plaque

& pant. I should say this
    all happens in the alley

behind our hardware job
    I should say he is forty

& I am not. how old am I?
    at the time I still had a curfew

know that. but back to his body
        his rank Hanes, overgrown

pubis, sour foreskin, the word
        natural at its bitter root.

what is semen but condensed cloud
        the body's recipe for lightning?

what is an ass but a canyon
        daring the tongue to jump?

what is a taint but hail
        that odd child of the sky?

my mouth is busy asking
        storm of flesh in front of me

I cast out my tongue like a key
        strung to a kite, wait for thunder.

POEMS IN WHICH ONE BLACK
MAN HOLDS ANOTHER

for Warith Taha, Charif Shanahan & Nate Marshall

i. faint

so the black boy falls into himself
& you mourn everyone ever
                        the breath between
what & happened filled with a second
line, mothers wrecked in black
                        boxes that call the boys
lover. the boy's is made of butterflies
his eyes flutter yellow & lift right off his face
                        his body a cocoon of no
a song suddenly empty, bones
like an afterthought, a missed prayer
                        a prayer, send it
to whatever god is near, watch
& know joy when his eyes, wing soft
                        return to his honeyed face
greet the boy back, jade embers
of god in his voice, *I'm fine, I'm fine*
                        believe until it's true

ii. fair

I believe God wasn't real until we made him so
I believe he muscled his way from our want
wet with our need to be unstarved, dishungered.
I believe the stars, their distant balled
night's great crescendo. I believe no night
spotted in milkhymns is without reason.
I believe tonight the reason is this boy
on my shoulder, a mess of black curl
& salt sorrow, crumbled to phoenix ash.

At the reading, the poet dedicates a poem
to the boy, reads him the history of his skin
& the boy is down. I catch. a pile of brother
a weeping of dust, boy in my arms
cinders remembering they are a bird
boy in my arms blue flame racing sky
boy in my arms a star & the space around
a bone bright shutter, & blacker still

iii. step

I am learning to follow a man's lead
& spin when he offers me wind

       it's in the kitchen, two black boys
       our fathers' music & a Sunday
       to sing away into light

I am learning to touch a man's back
& not think *saddle* or *conquer* or *burn*

       it's in your body, how it doesn't
       reduce mine to churned wet froth
       & tight, teethless tunnels

I am learning what loving a man is
not, that we don't have to end with blood

       it's in the lay of your hand
       on my shoulder, how it is
       not a fist, not a claw

I am learning what a brother is
how to touch & not scar or fuck

it's how you know the bodies
I devour & don't care, how you
don't want my body & don't care

I am learning to dance with my clothes on
to make fire in the absence of a storm

it's how we don't have sex
& never will, how the joy
is love enough

[AGAIN]

SONG OF THE WRECKAGE

"What is it you want me to reconcile myself to? I was born here almost 60 years ago, I'm not gonna live another 60 years. You always told me it takes time. It's taken my father's time, my mother's time, my uncle's time, my brother's & my sister's time, my niece's & my nephew's time . . . how much time do you want for your progress?"

—JAMES BALDWIN

I have no time for Red to be beautiful
with summer bloodied as it is & normal
as it's become, with the rusted, small bones
of boys who should be my father's age
buried under the beaming bones of boys
who should be my age, still tinged with meat.

I have no peace left, it's been replaced by smoke
& I am sick of always running from the fire
this time. I am sick with impossible hues of black
boys, their dark ghost, crow winged angels raised
lynch high off the ground. I mourn all the time
right out the sky. I got no need for the sun

& the moon might as well be a warning shot.
How many black boys stolen in the hot night?
From their own homes? From their own bodies?
How many black boys until we make history

finally let us in on the joke? How little progress
before it's not progress.? How much prayer & song

must we stuff our mouths with before we lose
our taste for empty? I got faith like a man down
in the dirt who don't believe in no kind of God
how he gonna watch the earth turn his legs to rot
how he got eternity to feel dirty & left behind
& wonder if there might be a land of light.

Surely, the end will begin with a drowning light.
A flash, atomic or squad car, has always meant we lose
& either blood & candles or ash & ash left behind.
When it goes down, cause the book says will go down,
let me watch the world make like my cousin & rot.
I got as much time to enjoy the burning as God.

Let me slow down this funeral-funk song,
the notes are all fucked in my head. I mean a boy was shot
& someone stopped the music, raised a glass, toasted progress
how the trees no longer bloom with sons, but the night
being a black thing is all I can guarantee of history.
I mean the rapture is our bodies, the buried bodies

chilled & emptied in the absence of the sun
the lives ended while Stevie played, gun smoke
mistaken for barbeque. I mean now has long been the time
look around, the end is too busy to bother with fire.
Not the flame, not the oceans, but first the taxes raised.
Then, dirty space where earth used to be, but first, black

must go. When enough people no longer beg for meat
convince them their power is choice. Call them beautiful
enough for them to believe you mean it. Then take the boys,
vanish the girls & don't tell a soul. Name it normal,
tell them keep the faith. They'll wait for some beast to claim his age
& not notice the end comes in votes, legislation, & eventually bones.

I have a dream that bones
stay clung to their meat
until a ripe old age
& you die ninety & beautiful
& the causes are more normal.
The dream has no black boys.

I dream of heat turning my black self black
but lately my dreams have no suns.
I dream of my fist raised
in a sea of nearby smoke
& of course I am on fire
my body out of flesh & time.

The dream is filled with trees filled with bodies.
No one thinks to start a song,
then I am studying 8th grade history
& somehow I've been shot
& marrow-hungry dogs chase me into night.
My wound is persistent, the blood makes progress

on my weight loss, I lose
so much, spoil with bullets, unsaved by light.
In heaven, I tell Sojourner not to look behind
urge the ancestors not to gaze down.
I never find him, but I'm sure God
doesn't need the info, I know he can smell the rot.

4 little girls burn up some, do the rest of their bodies rot?
If race isn't important, then why we concerned with who's behind?
                    If race is over, did we lose?

If I pay my tithes & my son still ain't breathing, what I owe God?
Is salvation only for white &/or the rich if it comes in the light?
                    How does the bottom keep falling down?

What did the poplar tree say to the bill about progress?
        By branch or by bill, they weigh the same, those black bodies.

Why don't we just celebrate our birthdays every midnight?
When the last time the world was saved by a song?

Who doesn't have the decency to ask forgiveness of the body they shot?
Has anyone every asked that last question to history?

When revolution is ready to come, who will have the time?

        Are you sick of the word *black*?

When can it be time for me to dress something in fire?
How bad are summers in the hood on the sun?

Cancer or Hollow Tip? How do you prefer your smoke?

In what broken home was America raised?

Better movie, *Boyz in the Hood* or *Scottsboro Boys*?

What is it with the dirt & bones?

                                        Define *normal*?

Who do the ants think has the best meat?

Please, will you show me something beautiful?

If I play dead, will I be acting my age?

Chaos has long come of age
with the boys who never stop being boys
& their pristine suits, coffins down right pretty.
An awful sky later revealed as earth jeweled with bones
I'm eating myself alive, though I said I'd give up meat
but if I am a child of my institutions, this is normal.

This is the destiny of a black child: raised
to lose virginities & minds & friends & time
in the fog that is a cloud that is smoke
over all the neighborhoods labeled black.
Someone is somewhere mourning their son.
Add one more stick to the fire.

If I am to believe in what you call history
then I can't believe in what you call progress.
Every hero I have ends up a liar or shot.
I stopped counting the ways to disappear bodies.
Sometimes all I need is music, other times fuck your song.
What is your blues juxtaposed to the black & ruby-wet of night?

I'll trouble the black corpse water, you make sure earth don't rot

or melt or burn up before we see if the roaches are behind

all this, hungry for their reign, hungry for us to lose

our minds & grill up the world. Or maybe it's God

& the Devil making bets in a room with low light

& God is too drunk to see that he's down.

& what about the boys down
in Jamaica, chopped & left to rot
under growing breadfruit & hot light?
Who know the lips they licked behind
church as the same that gave them up to God
& his church who sullied their hands & felt no loss.

what do we make of a nation, night
—colored & still with a sharp history
of blades where there should be song?
who can say the word progress
while standing in the field of unbodied bodies
the loose parts, the blood-drunk earth taking shots.

& what of Nigeria & her sugar-hungry fire
ready to drown the sweet child she raised?
My motherland is ruled by a dark sun
the clock's guilty hands the red-dry time
is always right for killing that which is black
& sinful. All around the world, smoke

rises from some poor man's body, his normal
organs & blood summon the vultures to sweet meat.
Is what's left a warning or an effigy? honey roasted bones
that still pine for a first kiss. These boys
poured all over the road, this new & darker age
where we burn all that ever call itself beautiful.

So me & the boys ride out to smoke
with Darrel, cause Darrel got that fire
& everything else: a blunt, a backseat, a black
& enough music to remind us we were raised
black in a era where our skin & sex is a time
bomb waiting to catapult us towards the sun.

I am not yet bold enough to call these boys beautiful.
I am an actor, I know how to blend in, look normal.
I know the pronouns to use when I talk about who bones
who in my backseat, I know there is never a proper age
to burn the closet down, but I want to kiss these boys
half in joy, half to touch them before we are good meat

for some police dog, before we gamble with summer & lose,
gunned down by an almost brother, a play cousin, luck down
the drain with the blood. If there is a (or in spite of?) God
let my small brown lips know their full brown lips before I rot
let us slow dance in the moonlight &, later, from behind
let us sway until we fade into a brown & endless light.

But that can't be. There are six of us, someone must get shot.
someone must never walk out of this night
someone must stop being a somebody & be one of the bodies
collected, scrapbooked, & misplaced by history.
Someone must go to college in the name of *progress*
& someone has to ready the drum for the war song.

What kind of jam should we play? What song
gets the apocalypse jumpin? When the sky gets shot
& the sun bleeds out, when the moon progresses
itself into either the ocean or deeper into night,
how should we dance at the end of history?
How bent should our knees be when they find the bodies?

The days are getting longer & I have no light.
Time no longer matters; we lose
them before we have them, the boys. Behind
the schoolhouse, with their fuzzy braids getting down
to the crude beat box of some who would let his teeth rot
before he stops the cipher. Do they know their name is God?

When the beast comes hungry for his day & his meat
let him find those boys, still 15 & beautiful
pray he has one small pity & he leaves them alone. Pray the boys
sing, with chaos all around, & finally have a chance to be normal.
Pray them suddenly 60, for so many black boys betrayed by age
never get to feel the settling of joints, the experience of bones.

Let them cypher until their song is the new sun,
give them a joint & let them build a world from smoke.
Let them build a black boy's world. Rhythm to replace time,
water free of the blood's salt, peaches where there was once fire,
watch the boy gods care for the dark child they raised
from nothingness, how it started black & ends black.

KING THE COLOR OF SPACE, TOWER OF MOLASSES & MARROW

I hear music rise off your skin. Each hair on your arm a tiny viola.
A wind full of bows blows & all I hear is the brown

hum of your flesh, a symphony of pigment too often drowned out
by the gun songs & sirens. Don't listen to that music.

You are the first light in the morning, the dark edge of the sun.
You are too beautiful for bullets. You, long the poster child for metal

wrecked bodies, are too precious for the dirt's greedy teeth.
You are what was left when the hot, bright stars danced

with the black endlessness around them. You are the scraps
of the beginning, you are not meant to end so soon.

I want to kiss you. Not on your mouth, but on your most
secret scars, your ashy black & journeyed knees,

your ring finger, the trigger finger, those hands
the world fears so much. I am not your enemy

not poison, not deadly sin, not ocean hungry for blood
nor trying to trick you. I came from the same red clay

same ship as you. You are my brother first, my lover
second & never a God. I am sick of people always

calling us Gods. What God do you know that dies this easy?
If I believed in fire, I would think you a thing scorched

& dangerous & glowing. But I no longer believe in embers
we know you can burn down with no flame for miles.

So thank you. Thank you for not fading to ash & memory.
Your existence is so kind.

ON GRACE

You know how when Usain Bolt runs
& you want to cry it's so beautiful? That.

How could we not be a song? I sing
this man in my bed all night, my mouth a loose choir
& his body a gospel & I don't mean like a song

I mean gospel like a religion or like a testimony
etched in gold. How could we be only a song?

I lay men down for what some call me a faggot for
but I call it *worship*, I see his wood & bark
Amen Amen Amen. I call out God's good name
in the midst of the first miracle—the black body.

Look at him, at us. Were the mountains not named
after some dark brotha's shoulders? Didn't the wind learn
its ways from watching two boys run the spine of a field?

Bless the birch-colored body, always threatening to grow
or burn. Bless the body that strikes fear in pale police
& wets the mouths of church girls & choir boys with want.

Am I allowed to say I praised my pastor most without the robe?
I have found God in the saltiest parts of men: the space between
the leg & what biology calls a man, the bottoms of feet, life's slow milk.

I watch the Heat play the Warriors & I am overcome by a need
for tears & teeth. I stopped playing football because being tackled
feels too much like making love. I pause in the middle of the street

watching the steady pace of the men on corners selling green
& all things dangerous & white. I watch the hands exchange money

& escape, the balancing act of hips & denim. This awful dance of poverty,
but the dancers? Tatted & callous ballerinas, henna dipped stars.

Do you know what it means to be that beautiful & still hunted
& still alive? Who knows this story but the elephants & the trees?

Who says the grace of a black man in motion is not perfect
as a tusk in the sun or a single leaf taking its sweet time to the ground?

ACKNOWLEDGMENTS

Thank you to the following editors at the following journals for publishing early versions of many of the poems contained in this book: *Anti-, Assaracus, Bloom Literary Journal, The Collagist, The Cortland Review, decomP Magazine, Devil's Lake Lit, Indiana Review, Joint Magazine, Kinfolks Journal, Knockout Magazine, Muzzle Magazine, Narrative Northeast, Orange Quarterly, PANK Magazine, The Paris American, Phantom Limb, Ploughshares, Poetry Magazine, Quarterly West, Radius Lit, Rhino Magazine, The Rumpus, Southern Indiana Review, Split This Rock's Poem of the Week, Sugar House Review, Tandem, Union Station Magazine, Vinyl, Weave Magazine.*

Thank you KMA Sullivan, Phillip B. Williams and the YesYes Books Team for believing in this work and helping bring it to life.

Thanks to all the friends, teachers, and mentors who helped shape these poems, supported me, and helped me find the peace I needed to write, especially Chris Walker, Amaud Johnson, Ron Wallace, Patricia Smith, Gabrielle Calvocoressi, Jericho Brown, Nate Marshall, Fatimah Asghar, Jamila Woods, Franny Choi, Aaron Samuels, Sam Sax, Hieu Minh Nguyen, Michael Lee, Blaire White, Karl Iglesias, Cydney Edwards, Angel Nafis, Morgan Parker, Tameka Cage Conley, Chinaka Hodge, Rafael Casal, Thiahera Nurse, Yolanda Pruitt, Nat Iosbaker & too many more.

Thanks to all the foundations whose support gave the time, space, and generosity gave to the building on this project, namely the faculty and family of Cave Canem & VONA, the support of the McKnight Foundation and the Poetry Foundation. Thank you to First Wave for providing a space to consistently challenge myself as an artist and to Jan Mandell & CTT for sparking this journey in that historic basement.

Lastly, thank you to my family. I don't know what this life would be like if I didn't have y'all to stand with.

DANEZ SMITH is the recipient of a 2014 Ruth Lilly & Dorothy Sargent Rosenberg Poetry Fellowship from Poetry Magazine & The Poetry Foundation. He is also the recipient of fellowships from the McKnight Foundation, Cave Canem, VONA, & elsewhere. Danez is the author of *[insert] Boy* (YesYes Books, 2014) & the chapbook *hands on ya knees* (Penmanship books, 2013). Danez is the winner of the 2014 Reading Series Contest sponsored by *The Paris-American* & was featured in The Academy of American Poets' Emerging Poets Series by Patricia Smith. Danez is a founding member of the multi-genre, multicultural Dark Noise Collective. His writing has appeared in *Poetry*, *Ploughshares*, *Beloit Poetry Journal*, *Kinfolks* & elsewhere. In Poetry Slam, he is a 2011 Individual World Poetry Slam finalist, the reigning two-time Rustbelt Individual Champion & was on 2014 Championship Team Sad Boy Supper Club. In 2014, he was the Festival Director for the Brave New Voices International Youth Poetry Slam. He holds a BA from UW-Madison where he was a First Wave Urban Arts Scholar. He was born in St. Paul, MN.

ALSO FROM YESYES BOOKS